This book is for you Walter.
Mamma loves you!

Hello cupcake!

*

LEILA LINDHOLM

NEW HOLLAND PUBLISHERS

Hello cupcake!

I fell in love with cupcakes for the first time when I moved to New York City when I was 21 years old. Cupcakes were everywhere and I especially remember the ones I used to buy from a snack van in Central Park. I'd been baking muffins since I was a child, but they were often a bit bigger and weren't garnished in any particular way, while it turned out that small, cute cupcakes came in an endless array of types in the US. A cupcake should be a bit firmer in consistency and not as crumbly as muffins. A cupcake is a bit like a sponge cake that you then glaze with frosting and you almost always put sprinkles and decorations on top.

In the US, people have been baking cupcakes like this since the 1950s and they've always been popular, but recently, there's been a surge of interest and cupcakes are now hotter than ever. The same is true of cupcake's buddy, the whoopie pie, which was created when a housewife took some leftover cupcake batter, put it on a baking tray, and baked it into big, flat cakes that she then put together in pairs with some marshmallow fluff in the middle. She pressed it all together like a macaron.

In this book, you'll find all my favourite recipes for cupcakes and whoopie pies and I hope you'll like them as much as I do!

Hugs, Leila

Contents

Sweet potato cupcakes

16 CUPCAKES

450 g (15 oz) sweet potato purée
  (1 large sweet potato)
3 free-range eggs
300 g (10½ oz) sugar
300 g (10½ oz) plain
  (all-purpose) flour
1 tsp vanilla extract
1½ tsp baking powder
1½ tsp ground cinnamon
1 tsp ground cardamom
½ tsp ground ginger
2 pinches salt
150 ml (5 fl oz) oil

CREAM CHEESE FROSTING

60 g (2 oz) softened butter
400g (14 oz) icing
  (confectioners') sugar
1 tsp vanilla extract
grated peel from 1 lime
150 g (5 oz) cream cheese

pumpkin seeds, for garnish

1. Turn the oven to 175°C (345°F).
2. Peel and cube the sweet potato. Boil the pieces in lightly salted water until soft. Pour off the water and mix the sweet potato into a smooth purée.
3. Whisk the eggs and sugar together until white and really fluffy.
4. Mix all the dry ingredients together and fold them into the eggs.
5. Add the oil and sweet potato purée.
6. Set out paper cups in a muffin tin and fill the cups until two-thirds full with the mixture.
7. Bake them in the middle of the oven for about 20-25 minutes. Put a toothpick in them to test them; they should not be sticky. Leave them to cool.

1. Mix together the butter, icing sugar, vanilla, grated lime peel and cream cheese.
2. Place a round nozzle on an icing bag and fill it with the frosting.
3. Frost the cupcakes and garnish with pumpkin seeds.

Blueberry lemon cupcakes

12 CUPCAKES

2 free-range eggs

150 g (5 oz) sugar

2 tsp vanilla extract

75 g (2½ oz) butter

75 ml (2¼ fl oz) milk

*275 g (9½ oz) plain
(all-purpose) flour*

1½ tsp baking powder

1 pinch salt

grated peel and juice from 2 lemons

250 g (9 oz) fresh blueberries

1. Turn the oven to 175°C (345°F).
2. Whisk the eggs, sugar and vanilla until white and really fluffy.
3. Melt the butter. Pour in the milk and mix it with the eggs.
4. Mix the flour, baking powder and salt together and carefully fold this into the egg mixture.
5. Mix in the grated peel and the lemon juice.
6. Set out paper cups in a muffin tin.
7. Layer the mixture with the blueberries and fill the cups until two-thirds full.
8. Bake them in the middle of the oven for about 15-20 minutes. Leave them to cool.

WHITE CHOCOLATE FROSTING

*200 g (7 oz) good-quality white
chocolate*

200 g (7 oz) cream cheese

1. Chop the chocolate and melt it in a water bath (in a bowl over boiling water). Let it cool down a bit.
2. Mix the chocolate with the cream cheese.
3. Frost the cupcakes, using a round nozzle.

Caramel cupcakes

12 CUPCAKES

3 free-range eggs
250 g (9 oz) sugar
1 tsp vanilla extract
350 g (12 oz) plain (all-purpose) flour
2 tsp baking powder
3 tbsp good-quality cocoa
1 pinch salt
50 g (1¾ oz) butter
100 ml (3½ fl oz) double cream
2 tbsp cold coffee
100 g (3½ oz) good-quality 70% dark chocolate

1 package choc-coated caramels

CHOCOLATE GANACHE FROSTING

250 g (9 oz) good-quality 70% dark chocolate
150 ml (5 fl oz) double cream
2 tsp golden syrup
1 pinch sea salt
1 tbsp butter
100 g (3½ oz) cream cheese

1. Turn the oven to 175°C (345°F).
2. Whisk the eggs, sugar and vanilla until white and really fluffy.
3. Mix the flour, baking powder, cocoa and salt and fold it carefully into the egg mixture.
4. Melt the butter and mix it with the cream.
5. Mix this into the eggs and add the coffee.
6. Coarsely chop the chocolate and melt it in a water bath (in a bowl over boiling water).
7. Add the chocolate to the mixture.
8. Set out paper cups in a muffin tin and fill the cups until two-thirds full.
9. Press two caramels into each cup.
10. Bake them in the middle of the oven for about 15 minutes. Leave them to cool.

1. Finely chop the chocolate in a mixer.
2. Boil the cream, syrup and salt and pour it over the chocolate while mixing it. Add the butter and cream cheese and pulse (press on and off, on and off). Note: Only mix it until it's mixed together. If you mix it too much, it will separate.
3. Frost the cupcakes, using a star nozzle.

Chocolate swirl cheesecake cupcakes

16 CUPCAKES

BISCUIT BASE

400 g (14 oz) digestive biscuits
150 g (5 oz) butter

CHEESECAKE MIXTURE

600 g (21 oz) cream cheese
875 ml (30 fl oz) quark
150 g (5 oz) sugar
2 tsp vanilla extract
4 free-range eggs
100 ml (3½ fl oz) double cream

CHOCOLATE SWIRL

150 g (5 oz) good-quality 60% dark
   chocolate
3 tbsp espresso

TOPPING

200 ml (7 fl oz) crème fraîche
300 ml (10½ fl oz) double cream

1. Turn the oven to 150°C (300°F).
2. Finely crush the biscuits in a mixer (or put them in a plastic bag and crush them with a rolling pin).
3. Melt the butter and mix it with the biscuit pieces.
4. Set out paper cups in a muffin tin and divide the biscuits amongst them.
5. In a bowl, whip the cream cheese and quark until creamy.
6. Mix in the sugar and vanilla.
7. Mix in one egg at a time and finally add the cream.
8. Break the chocolate in pieces and melt it in a water bath (in a bowl over boiling water). Mix in the coffee.
9. Mix half of the cheesecake mixture with the chocolate.
10. Swirl the mixtures into the cups with a spoon.
11. Bake for about 25 minutes. They should be firm but can jiggle a bit. Leave them to cool and then chill them in the refrigerator until they are refrigerator-cold.
12. Mix the crème fraîche and cream and whip them until fluffy with an electric mixer. Put some on top of each cupcake.

THIS IS A FILLING CHEESECAKE CUPCAKE FOR ALL CHEESECAKE-LOVERS. IT IS
IMPORTANT TO CHOOSE A CHOCOLATE THAT DOESN'T HAVE TOO HIGH A COCOA
PERCENTAGE SO THAT THE CUPCAKE ISN'T TOO BITTER (70% CHOCOLATE IS OFTEN
TOO BITTER). I USUALLY SERVE THEM WITH FRESH BERRIES.

The cupcake story...

In the US, people have been baking cupcakes for over 100 years, but it was in the 1950s that there was a big surge of interest! I've always been a big fan of that historical period and I've been inspired by it. After I moved to New York City I discovered cupcakes and fell in love with them. It was the look that I liked the most, because they often bake cupcakes from a mix. I became inspired and started baking cupcakes at home with real butter and fresh ingredients.

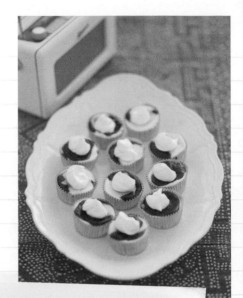

I ♥ cupcakes!

What I really love about cupcakes is that they can be varied with beautiful decorations and different tastes. There isn't a right or a wrong; what's most important is that they're tasty!

Sticky pecan upside-down cupcakes

12 CUPCAKES

PECAN CARAMEL

50 g (1¾ oz) butter

2 tbsp honey

50 g (1¾ oz) brown sugar

300 g (10½ oz) pecans

melted butter, to brush on the cups

CUPCAKES

2 free-range eggs

150 g (5 oz) sugar

1 tsp vanilla extract

75 g (2½ oz) butter

50 ml (1¾ fl oz) milk

250 g (9 oz) plain (all-purpose) flour

1½ tsp baking powder

½ tsp ground cinnamon

1 pinch ground cloves

1 pinch salt

1. Turn the oven to 175°C (345°F).
2. Start with the caramel. Melt the butter, honey and brown sugar in a saucepan while stirring it for a couple of minutes, until it turns into a caramel. Remove it from the heat.
3. Halve the pecans lengthwise.
4. Set out paper cups in a muffin tin and brush them with the melted butter.
5. Put just 1 tablespoon of caramel in each cup and distribute the pecans over the caramel.
6. Whisk the eggs, sugar and vanilla until white and really fluffy.
7. Melt the butter, add the milk and mix it into the egg mixture.
8. Mix the flour, baking powder, cinnamon, cloves and salt together and carefully fold this into the egg mixture.
9. Pour the mixture over the pecans. Bake them in the middle of the oven for about 15 minutes. Leave them to cool a bit and then turn them upside-down. Carefully pull off the paper before they have cooled.

THESE WONDERFUL, TASTY AND MOIST CAKES ARE MY FAVOURITES. YOU MAKE THEM IN
PAPER MUFFIN CUPS IN A MUFFIN TRAY AND PUT THE PECAN CARAMEL IN THE BOTTOM.
YOU SPOON CUPCAKE BATTER OVER THAT AND THEN BAKE THEM IN THE OVEN. WHEN YOU
TAKE OUT THE CUPCAKES AND THEY'RE STILL WARM, YOU REMOVE THE PAPER. I BAKE THEM
OFTEN THROUGHOUT THE YEAR, BUT THEY'RE PARTICULARLY GOOD TO SERVE AT CHRISTMAS
BECAUSE THEY HAVE A SPICY FLAVOUR.

Fourth of July cupcakes

12 CUPCAKES
2 free-range eggs
150 g (5 oz) sugar
1 tsp vanilla extract
75 g (2½ oz) butter
75 ml (2½ fl oz) milk
275 g (9½ oz) plain (all-purpose)
  flour
1½ tsp baking powder
1 pinch salt
grated peel and juice from 3 limes
200 g (7 oz) fresh blueberries
200 g (7 oz) fresh raspberries

CREAM CHEESE FROSTING
60 g (2 oz) softened butter
400 g (14 oz) icing sugar
1 tsp vanilla extract
1 tbsp freshly squeezed lime juice
100 g (3½ oz) cream cheese

flags, blueberries and raspberries,
  for garnish

1. Turn the oven to 175°C (345°F).
2. Whisk the eggs, sugar and vanilla until white and really fluffy.
3. Melt the butter, add the milk and then mix it with the egg mixture.
4. Mix the flour, baking powder and salt together and carefully fold this into the eggs.
5. Mix in the grated peel and juice from the limes.
6. Set out paper cups in a muffin tin.
7. Layer the blueberries, raspberries and dough mixture in the cups. Fill them two-thirds full.
8. Bake them in the middle of the oven for about 15–20 minutes. Leave them to cool.

1. Whip the butter, sugar, vanilla, lime juice and cream cheese until creamy.
2. Spread the frosting on the cakes and garnish with flags and berries.

CELEBRATING THE FOURTH OF JULY IS A BIG DEAL IN THE US. THEY OFTEN CELEBRATE
WITH A BARBEQUE ON THE GRASS AND, OF COURSE, ALONG WITH THIS YOU HAVE TO
HAVE BAKED GOODS IN THE COLOURS OF THE AMERICAN FLAG.

Peanut butter whoopie pies

20 WHOOPIE PIES

3 free-range eggs
250 g (9 oz) sugar
1 tsp vanilla extract
50 g (1¾ oz) butter
100 ml (2¾ fl oz) sour cream
2 tbsp cold coffee
350 g (12 oz) plain (all-purpose) flour
2 tsp baking powder
4 tbsp good-quality cocoa
1 pinch salt
100 g (3½ oz) good-quality 70%
  dark chocolate

1. Turn the oven to 175°C (345°F).
2. Whisk the eggs, sugar and vanilla until white and really fluffy.
3. Melt the butter, add the sour cream and coffee and mix this into the eggs.
4. Mix the flour, baking powder, cocoa and salt, and carefully fold this into the egg mixture.
5. Coarsely chop the dark chocolate and melt it in a water bath (in a bowl over boiling water). Mix it with the other ingredients.
6. Pipe or spoon out the mixture onto baking paper with a tablespoon.
7. Bake them in batches in the middle of the oven for about 10 minutes. Leave them to cool completely. Meanwhile, make the peanut butter frosting.

PEANUT BUTTER FROSTING

50 g (1¾ oz) softened peanut butter
250 g (9 oz) icing sugar
2 tbsp good-quality cocoa
1 tsp vanilla extract
100 g (3½ oz) cream cheese
1 tbsp warm coffee

salted peanuts, for garnish

1. Blend the peanut butter, icing sugar, cocoa, vanilla and cream cheese together until creamy. Add the coffee and whip the frosting with an electric mixer.
2. Fill an icing bag and use a round nozzle.
3. Pipe the frosting onto the underside of one cake and put it together with another cake (without frosting), like a macaron. Pipe a little frosting on top and garnish with peanuts.

Mississippi mud cupcakes

12 CUPCAKES

2 free-range eggs
250 g (9 oz) sugar
1 tsp vanilla extract
350 g (12 oz) plain (all-purpose) flour
1 tsp bicarbonate of soda
  (baking soda)
1 pinch salt
200 g (7 oz) good-quality 70%
  dark chocolate
100 g (3½ oz) butter
2 tbsp strong coffee

1. Turn the oven to 175°C (345°F).
2. Whisk the eggs, sugar and vanilla until white and really fluffy.
3. Mix the flour, bicarbonate of soda and salt in a mixing bowl.
4. Coarsely chop the dark chocolate and melt it in a water bath (in a bowl over boiling water).
5. Melt the butter and add the coffee.
6. Carefully fold everything together.
7. Set out paper cups in a muffin tin. Fill them two-thirds full.
8. Bake them in the middle of the oven for about 10 minutes. They should sink in the middle after you take them out of the oven. Leave them to cool.

FUDGE GLAZE

125 ml (4 fl oz) double cream
200 ml (7 fl oz) milk
2 tsp golden syrup
100 g (3½ oz) good-quality 70%
  dark chocolate

whipped cream and maraschino
  cherries, for garnish

1. Boil the cream, milk and syrup in a saucepan. Remove from the heat and leave to cool for a little while.
2. Finely chop the dark chocolate, put the pieces in the saucepan and stir until smooth. Let it cool a bit and then pour it into the valley in the middle of the cupcakes.
3. Garnish with lightly whipped cream and a maraschino cherry.

THIS IS MY VERSION OF THE AMERICAN MISSISSIPPI MUD CAKE. IN THE US, IT'S OFTEN SERVED WITH A FLOOD OF CREAMY CARAMEL ON TOP AND SOMETIMES WITH CHOCOLATE SAUCE, CARAMEL SAUCE AND MARSHMALLOWS AS WELL. THERE ARE SURELY THOUSANDS OF VARIATIONS ON HOW IT CAN BE BAKED AND SERVED...THIS IS HOW I LIKE IT BEST.

Gone to the
beach...

The beach is my son Walter's paradise. We spend hours on the sand while Walter bakes his own sand cakes. It's good to bring along something to snack on.

Une journée sur la plage...

We spend the summer in Montalivet in France. Here we sun-bathe, swim, fly kites and look for treasure on the beach. We always bring a well-filled picnic basket with us. In it, there is a drink or soup in a thermos (so it stays warm all day) and cupcakes and whoopie pies in my little cake tin with an icepack.

Look, mamma!!

Of course, we also take a good lunch with us. In France, there's unbelievable bread and fantastic raw ingredients for salads. You can't live on cupcakes alone!

Bounty cupcakes

12 CUPCAKES

100 g (3½ oz) coconut flakes
100 g (3½ oz) good-quality 70%
   dark chocolate
2 free-range eggs
150 g (5 oz) sugar
1 tsp vanilla extract
250 g (9 oz) plain (all-purpose) flour
1½ tsp baking powder
1 pinch salt
100 g (3½ oz) butter
75 ml (2½ fl oz) coconut milk
2½ tbsp good-quality cocoa
1½ tbsp cold coffee
1 tbsp Malibu (coconut liqueur)
6 Bounty or Mounds bars

1. Turn the oven to 175°C (345°C).
2. Toast the coconut flakes in a dry frying pan until they have lightly browned.
3. Coarsely chop the dark chocolate and melt it in a water bath (in a bowl over boiling water).
4. Whisk the eggs, sugar and vanilla until white and really fluffy.
5. Mix the flour, bicarbonate of soda and salt and carefully fold it into the egg mixture.
6. Melt the butter, add the coconut milk and mix into the egg mixture.
7. Stir in the melted chocolate, the toasted coconut flakes, the cocoa, coffee and Malibu.
8. Set out paper cups in a muffin tin and fill them two-thirds full.
9. Halve the Bounty bars and stick one half into each cupcake.
10. Bake them in the middle of the oven for about 12 minutes. Leave them to cool.

BOUNTY GLAZE

250 g (9 oz) good-quality 70%
   dark chocolate
150 ml (5 fl oz) double cream
2 tbsp honey
1 pinch sea salt
1 tbsp butter
100 g (3½ oz) cream cheese

coconut flakes, for garnish

1. Finely chop the chocolate in a mixer.
2. Boil the cream, honey and salt and pour it over the chocolate while mixing it. Add the butter and cream cheese and pulse (turn it on and off, on and off). Note: mix only until the cream has come together; if you mix it for too long, it will separate.
3. Spread the frosting over the cupcakes.
4. Garnish with coconut flakes.

I'M CHILDISH IN THAT I LOVE HAVING SWEETS IN MY BAKED GOODS AND
THIS IS PROBABLY ONE OF MY MOST SUCCESSFUL RECIPES. IF YOU LIKE
COCONUT, YOU MUST BAKE THESE CUPCAKES. THEY'RE TO-DIE-FOR!

Rocky road cupcakes

12 CUPCAKES

3 free-range eggs
250 g (9 oz) sugar
1 tsp vanilla extract
50 g (1¾ oz) butter
100 ml (3½ fl oz) sour cream
2 tbsp cold coffee
350 g (12 oz) plain (all-purpose) flour
2 tsp baking powder
4 tbsp good-quality cocoa
1 pinch salt
100 g (3½ oz) good-quality 70%
   dark chocolate
2 handfuls choc-coated caramels
2 handfuls mini marshmallows
200 g (7 oz) salted peanuts

1. Turn the oven to 175°C (345°F).
2. Whisk the eggs, sugar and vanilla until white and
   really fluffy.
3. Melt the butter, add the sour cream and coffee and
   mix it with the egg mixture.
4. Mix the flour, baking powder, cocoa and salt and
   carefully fold this mixture into the eggs.
5. Coarsely chop the dark chocolate and melt it in a
   water bath (in a bowl over boiling water).
6. Add the chocolate to the rest of the ingredients.
7. Set out paper cups in a muffin tin and layer the batter,
   the choc-coated caramels, mini marshmallows and
   peanuts in them. Fill them two-thirds full.
8. Bake them in the middle of the oven for about
   15 minutes. Leave them to cool.

FUDGE GLAZE

150 ml (5 oz) double cream
50 ml (1¾ fl oz) milk
2 tbsp honey
200 g (7 oz) good-quality 70%
   dark chocolate
1 tbsp butter

choc-coated caramels, salted
   peanuts and mini marshmallows, for
   garnish

1. Boil the cream, milk and honey in a saucepan. Remove
   from the heat and let it cool a little.
2. Finely chop the chocolate and mix it into the warm
   milk so the chocolate melts. Stir in the butter.
3. Spoon some glaze onto the middle of each cupcake
   and garnish with small pieces of choc-coated
   caramels, peanuts and mini marshmallows.

Sweet MEMORIES...

One of my strongest food-related memories is when I stood on a little stool in my grandma's kitchen and spooned batter into muffin tins. Grandma and I created masterpieces in the oven and she even let me lick the bowl! I was probably just three years old, but I remember it so strongly. That's what's so wonderful about baking with your children and grandchildren. We are creating memories for life and at the same time we're doing something creative and fun together. Also, we can eat and offer others our delicious homemade creations without worrying about any strange additives. That's why I've decided that this is something I want to share with and give to my children and I really hope I can inspire others to do so too. Walter often talks about how Mamma bakes and, of course, you can understand why. He loves baking too, which bodes well. It's a real gift to be able to bake and cook. The best way to get to eat good food is to learn to make it yourself. That's why it can be a good idea to allow children to get familiar with the kitchen and to create that magic early in their lives...

Rhubarb cheesecake cupcakes

16 CUPCAKES

RHUBARB COMPOTE
½ litre (17 fl oz) sliced rhubarb
200 g (7 oz) sugar

BISCUIT BASE
400 g (14 oz) digestive biscuits
150 g (5 oz) butter

CHEESECAKE BATTER
300 g (10½ oz) cream cheese
175 ml (6 fl oz) quark
50 g (1¾ oz) sugar
50 g (1¾ oz) cornstarch (cornflour)
1 tsp vanilla extract
2 free-range eggs
50 ml (1¾ fl oz) double cream
100 g (3½ oz) good-quality white
 chocolate

whipped cream and fresh
 raspberries, for garnish

1. Turn the oven to 150°C (300°F).
2. Cook the rhubarb with the sugar (no water is needed as the rhubarb has so much water in it). Cook for about 20 minutes, until the rhubarb is soft. Stir carefully.
3. Crumble the digestive biscuits in a mixer.
4. Melt the butter and mix it with the biscuit crumbs.
5. Set out paper cups in a muffin tin and put biscuits in the bottom of each cup.
6. Whip the cream cheese and quark until creamy.
7. Mix in the sugar, cornstarch and vanilla.
8. Mix in the eggs and finally the cream.
9. Chop the dark chocolate and melt it in a water bath (in a bowl over boiling water).
10. Fold the rhubarb compote into the cheesecake mixture and fill the muffin cups.
11. Bake for about 25 minutes.
12. Store them somewhere cold and serve cold with a little whipped cream and fresh raspberries.

MY RHUBARB CHEESECAKE CUPCAKES ARE A REAL TREAT THAT NEVER DISAPPOINT ANYONE. THE COMPOTE IS REALLY EASY TO MAKE, AS IS THE CHEESECAKE BATTER. IF YOU WANT, YOU CAN MAKE CHEESECAKE CUPCAKES WITH OTHER FLAVOURINGS, SUCH AS WITH MIXED BERRIES OR BLUEBERRIES. SWIRL THE BERRIES WITH THE BATTER IN THE MUFFIN CUPS.

Saffron cupcakes

12 CUPCAKES

3 free-range eggs
250 g (9 oz) sugar
1 tsp vanilla extract
100 g (3½ oz) butter
½ g (1 sachet) saffron
100 ml (3½ fl oz) double cream
350 g (12 oz) plain (all-purpose) flour
2 tsp baking powder
1 pinch salt
1 tbsp light rum

1. Turn the oven to 175°C (345°F).
2. Whisk the eggs, sugar and vanilla until white and really fluffy.
3. Melt the butter with the saffron. Mix in the cream and boil. Mix with the eggs.
4. Mix the flour, baking powder and salt together and carefully fold this into the egg mixture.
5. Flavour with rum.
6. Set out paper cups in a muffin tin and fill the cups until two-thirds full with the mixture.
7. Bake them in the middle of the oven for about 15-20 minutes.

CREAM CHEESE FROSTING

60 g (2 oz) softened butter
400 g (14 oz) icing sugar
1 tsp vanilla extract
1 tbsp freshly squeezed lemon juice
100 g (3½ oz) cream cheese

sprinkles, for garnish

1. Mix the butter, icing sugar, vanilla, lemon juice and cream cheese until creamy.
2. Spread the frosting on the cupcakes.
3. Garnish with sprinkles.

I USUALLY BAKE THESE FOR CHRISTMAS AND EASTER. CHILDREN OFTEN CALL THEM 'DUCK MUFFINS' BECAUSE OF THE GORGEOUS BIRD-YELLOW COLOUR. YOU CAN ALSO GARNISH THEM WITH A LITTLE GROUND CINNAMON INSTEAD OF SPRINKLES.

Chocolate and lavender cupcakes

12 CUPCAKES

3 free-range eggs

250 g (9 oz) sugar

1 tsp vanilla extract

350 g (12 oz) plain (all-purpose) flour

2 tsp baking powder

3 tbsp good-quality cocoa

1 pinch salt

50 g (1¾ oz) butter

100 ml (3½ fl oz) double cream

3 fresh lavender flowers (or ½ tsp dried lavender)

2 tbsp cold coffee

100 g (3½ oz) good-quality 70% dark chocolate

1. Turn the oven to 175°C (345°F).
2. Whisk the eggs, sugar and vanilla until white and really fluffy.
3. Mix the flour, baking powder, cocoa and salt and carefully fold into the egg mixture.
4. Warm the butter, cream and lavender. Let it steep for a few moments and then strain out the lavender flowers.
5. Mix this with the egg mixture and add the cold coffee.
6. Coarsely chop the dark chocolate and melt it in a water bath (in a bowl over boiling water).
7. Add the chocolate to the batter.
8. Set out paper cups in a muffin tin and fill the cups until two-thirds full with the mixture.
9. Bake them in the middle of the oven for about 15 minutes. Leave them to cool.

CHOCOLATE AND LAVENDER FROSTING

250 g (9 oz) good-quality 70% dark chocolate

150 ml (5 oz) double cream

3 fresh lavender flowers (or ½ tsp dried lavender)

2 tbsp honey

2 pinches sea salt

1 tbsp butter

100 g (3½ oz) cream cheese

lavender flowers, for garnish

1. Finely chop the chocolate in a mixer.
2. Boil the cream, lavender, honey and sea salt and pour it over the chocolate while stirring it.
3. Add the butter and cream cheese and pulse (press on and off, on and off). Note: only mix it until it's mixed together. If you mix it too much, it will separate.
4. Using an icing bag with a round nozzle, frost the cupcakes. Garnish with lavender flowers.

CHOCOLATE AND LAVENDER ARE A WONDERFUL AND PERHAPS UNEXPECTED COMBINATION.
SOMETIMES I FLAVOUR MY CHOCOLATE CAKE WITH FRESH LAVENDER FLOWERS. IT'S ALSO
DELICIOUS TO MAKE A LAVENDER SUGAR BY MIXING FRESH LAVENDER FLOWERS WITH SUGAR AND
SERVING IT ON STRAWBERRIES.

Key lime pie cupcakes

16 CUPCAKES

BISCUIT BASE
400 g (14 oz) digestive biscuits
125 g (4 oz) melted butter

FILLING
2 tins (800 g/28 oz) sweetened
* condensed milk*
8 free-range yolks
grated peel and juice from 10 limes

whipped cream and lime, to serve

1. Turn the oven to 175°C (345°F).
2. Crumble the digestive biscuits in a mixer and mix them with the melted butter.
3. Set out paper cups in a muffin tin and press biscuits in the bottom and around the sides of each cup.
4. Pre-bake the biscuit base in the oven for about 10 minutes. Leave to cool.
5. Mix the condensed milk with the egg yolks, grated lime peel and lime juice. Let steep for at least 30-60 minutes. Strain through a fine strainer and throw away all the peels.
6. Pour the filling over the biscuit base and bake in the middle of the oven for about 25 minutes. Leave them to cool completely and serve with whipped cream and slices of lime.

KEY LIME IS A LITTLE SWEET-SOUR FRUIT FROM KEY WEST, A PENINSULA OUTSIDE MIAMI IN THE US. THE PIE HAS BECOME ALMOST LEGENDARY AND THERE ARE MANY FIRM OPINIONS ABOUT HOW IT SHOULD BE MADE. I THINK IT'S BEST WHEN YOU MAKE IT WITH SWEETENED CONDENSED MILK.

Butterfly lemon cupcakes

12 CUPCAKES

3 free-range eggs
250 g (9 oz) sugar
1 tsp vanilla extract
100 g (3½ oz) butter
100 ml (3½ fl oz) sour cream
400 g (14 oz) plain (all-purpose) flour
2 tsp baking powder
1 pinch salt
100 g (3½ oz) poppy seeds
grated peel of 3 and juice of
  2 lemons

1. Turn the oven to 175°C (345°F).
2. Whisk the eggs, sugar and vanilla until white and really fluffy.
3. Melt the butter, add the sour cream and mix with the egg mixture.
4. Mix the flour, baking powder, salt and poppy seeds and carefully fold into the mixture.
5. Mix in the grated peel and lemon juice.
6. Set out paper cups in a muffin tin and fill the cups until two-thirds full with the mixture.
7. Bake them in the middle of the oven for about 15 minutes. Leave them to cool.

LEMON CREAM

3 lemons
150 g (5 oz) sugar
50 g (1¾ oz) butter
2 tbsp cornstarch (cornflour)
2 free-range eggs
2 free-range yolks
150 ml (5 fl oz) double cream

1. Heat the juice from two lemons and the grated peel from three with the sugar and butter.
2. Strain and throw out the peel.
3. Mix the cornstarch with the juice from the third lemon and add to the warm mixture.
4. Whisk the eggs and yolks.
5. Add the eggs to the mixture and simmer over heat until the cream has thickened.
6. Pour the cream into a bowl and leave to cool completely.
7. Whip the cream until fluffy and fold it together with the cool lemon cream.
8. Slice the top off every cupcake and halve the top. Cut little lines into the sides.
9. Using a teaspoon, scoop out a little of the cupcake and fill the hole with lemon cream.
10. Place the halved top over the cream like wings.

Celebrate a child's birthday with a party—it is usually really important to them. Of course, it's extra fun if they get to help with the baking and other activities in the kitchen. Also, it's wonderful to be able to have creative quality time with your children—you can create magic in the kitchen with eggs, sugar, baking powder, butter, milk and flour!

Party tips...

You can freeze cupcakes if you want to prepare them a
few days before the party. They should be cooled completely
before you freeze them and they should be frozen fresh and
well-wrapped in plastic. Then take them out and defrost them
completely before you top them with frosting. If they aren't
completely defrosted, there is a chance that the frosting might
melt from the moisture in the cupcakes.

You can prepare the frosting
and keep it in the refrigerator
overnight. Just whip it again
before frosting the cupcakes.
This doesn't work for frosting
that includes melted chocolate, as it
gets too hard.

Mix and match! I like to use both old and new things when setting the table. Doing so creates a nice feeling and character. Don't be scared to try different colours and patterns.

Lovely Jane!

Yummy...

Make napkins from your favourite material or scraps with crafting scissors. The napkins may not last forever, but they'll be fun for the party.

Cut out crowns from gold paper. Tape them together and add a piece of elastic that goes under the chin.

Three types of cakes! For my cupcake parties, I usually make three different types of cupcakes. They are like small, cute individual cakes with different flavours, so you can be pretty sure that everyone will be satisfied. But cupcakes aren't just for kids. You can also offer them on other occasions, such as afternoon teas, weddings, christenings, Easter, graduation parties, Christmas and birthdays.

I love beautiful cake dishes and I think they really make the party. If you have different levels on the table, it makes things seem more festive than if everything is at the same height.

Flags! It's easy to make nice little flags for the cupcakes. All you need are cocktail sticks, coloured paper, glue and scissors. I like to cut an oblong strip, put glue on one side and then fold it over the cocktail stick. Then I cut out the shape of a flag. Sometime I make a strip in another colour, so the flag has two colours.

Banoffee whoopie pies

12 WHOOPIE PIES
100 g (3½ oz) softened butter
150 g (5 oz) sugar
350 g (12 oz) plain (all-purpose) flour
2 tsp vanilla extract
1 tsp baking powder
1 tsp bicarbonate of soda
  (baking soda)
1 free-range egg
100 ml (3½ fl oz) double cream
50 g (1¾ oz) walnuts

CARAMEL SAUCE
250 ml (9 fl oz) double cream
50 g (1¾ oz) sugar
100 ml (3½ fl oz) golden syrup

FILLING
300 ml (10½ fl oz) double cream
2 bananas

1. Turn the oven to 175°C (345°F).
2. Whisk the butter and sugar until creamy.
3. Mix the dry ingredients and fold them into the batter.
4. Mix in the egg and cream and stir into a smooth batter.
5. Pipe or spoon out the mixture onto baking paper with a tablespoon.
6. Place a walnut half in half of the cakes (these will be the tops of the whoopie pies)
7. Bake them in batches in the middle of the oven for about 10 minutes.
8. Make the caramel. Mix the cream, sugar and syrup in a heavy-bottomed saucepan and cook the caramel for about 20 minutes. Leave to cool.
9. Whip the cream for the filling until fluffy.
10. Slice the bananas. Place a spoonful of whipped cream on a whoopie bottom (the half without walnut), drizzle with caramel sauce, place two slices of bananas on it, and drizzle with more caramel. Add the top of the whoopie pie (the half with the walnut).

HOW DO YOU KNOW WHEN CARAMEL IS READY? CHILL A PLATE IN THE FREEZER. PUT A
SPOONFUL OF CARAMEL ON THE PLATE TO TEST THE CONSISTENCY. THE LONGER YOU COOK
THE SAUCE, THE THICKER IT WILL BE.

Mazarin cupcakes with fresh berries

16 CUPCAKES

250 g (9 oz) softened butter
500 g (17½ oz) almond paste
5 free-range eggs
100 g (3½ oz) plain (all-purpose)
  flour

TOPPING

500 g (17½ oz) double cream
2 litres (70 fl oz) berries
  (strawberries, cherries or
  raspberries)

1. Turn the oven to 175°C (345°F).
2. Whip the butter and grated almond paste until creamy.
3. Add an egg, one at a time, while continuing to whip.
4. Fold in the flour last.
5. Set out paper cups in a muffin tin and fill the cups until two-thirds full with the mixture.
6. Bake them in the middle of the oven for about 20 minutes. Leave them to cool completely.
7. Whip the cream until fluffy and slice the berries.
8. Pipe the cream on the cakes so it looks like a little beehive and top with berries.

THIS MOIST ALMOND CAKE WAS PROBABLY NAMED AFTER A LEGENDARY FRENCH CARDINAL. IT IS OFTEN SERVED WITH A SUGAR ICING AND SOMETIMES RASPBERRY JAM (AND IS THEN CALLED CATALAN). MAZARINS SHOULD BE HEAVY AND MOIST AND THEY SHOULD CONTAIN LOTS OF ALMONDS AND BUTTER. DON'T BAKE THEM FOR TOO LONG OR THEY'LL BE DRY.

Easter cupcakes

12 CUPCAKES
2 free-range eggs
150 g (5 oz) sugar
100 g (3½ oz) hazelnuts
150 g (5 oz) plain (all-purpose) flour
1 tsp baking powder
75 ml (2½ fl oz) milk

1. Turn the oven to 175°C (345°F).
2. Whisk the eggs and sugar until white and really fluffy.
3. Pulverise the nuts in a mixer or grind them.
4. Mix the nuts, flour and baking powder and fold into the egg mixture.
5. Add the milk.
6. Set out paper cups in a muffin tin and fill the cups until two-thirds full with the mixture.
7. Bake them in the middle of the oven for about 20 minutes. Test them with a toothpick; they shouldn't be sticky. Leave them to cool.

NUTELLA FROSTING
100 g (3½ oz) Nutella
400 g (14 oz) icing (confectioners') sugar
4 tbsp good-quality cocoa
2 tsp vanilla extract
150 g (5 oz) cream cheese
1 tbsp coffee

1. Mix the Nutella, icing sugar, cocoa, vanilla and cream cheese until creamy.
2. Add the coffee and whip until fluffy.
3. Spread the frosting on the cakes.
4. Squeeze the almond paste through a garlic press.
5. Shape the threads into a small nest on top of the frosting.
6. Place a few chocolate eggs in each nest.

NEST
400 g (14 oz) almond paste
36 small chocolate eggs

I USUALLY BAKE THESE NUTTY AND MOIST CUPCAKES AT EASTER. YOU CAN, OF COURSE, MAKE THEM AT ANY TIME OF THE YEAR, AND THEN YOU CAN FILL THE NESTS WITH SOMETHING ELSE, SUCH AS BERRIES OR ANOTHER SWEET.

Walter's birthday cupcakes

12 CUPCAKES

3 free-range eggs
250 g (9 oz) sugar
1 tsp vanilla extract
100 g (3½ oz) butter
100 ml (3½ fl oz) milk
350 g (12 oz) flour
2 tsp baking powder
1 pinch salt
grated peel and juice from 3 limes

1. Turn the oven to 175°C (345°F).
2. Whisk the eggs, sugar and vanilla until white and really fluffy.
3. Melt the butter, add the milk and mix with the eggs.
4. Mix the flour, baking powder and salt and carefully fold this into the egg mixture.
5. Mix in the grated peel and juice from the limes.
6. Set out paper cups in a muffin tin and fill the cups until two-thirds full with the mixture.
7. Bake them in the middle of the oven for about 15 minutes. Leave them to cool.

CREAM CHEESE FROSTING

60 g (2 oz) softened butter
400 g (14 oz) icing (confectioners') sugar
1 tsp vanilla extract
grated peel from 3 limes
150 g (5 oz) cream cheese

sprinkles and candles, to garnish

1. Whip the butter, icing sugar, vanilla, grated lime peel and cream cheese until really fluffy.
2. Spread the frosting on the cakes and garnish with sprinkles. Put candles in the cakes.

The whoopie story...

Small, cute whoopie pies were created in the 1920s in Maine, which is in the Amish country in the US. The legend claims that the cake got its name because children shouted 'whoopie!' when they found these sweet treats in their lunchboxes. Whoopie pies were initially made with marshmallow fluff but over the years many fillings have been developed.

Tip! I often colour the frosting in different colours or flavour it in different ways, such as with chocolate, spices, coconut, nuts, peanut butter or Nutella. You can also roll the cupcakes with frosting in sprinkles, which is a job children often like to have...

Nutella whoopie pies

20 WHOOPIE PIES

3 free-range eggs

250 g (9 oz) sugar

1 tsp vanilla extract

50 g (1¾ oz) butter

100 ml (3½ fl oz) sour cream

2 tbsp cold coffee

350 g (12 oz) plain (all-purpose) flour

2 tsp baking powder

4 tbsp good-quality cocoa powder

1 pinch salt

100 g (3½ oz) good-quality 70%
   dark chocolate

NUTELLA FROSTING

100 g (3½ oz) Nutella

400 g (14 oz) icing (confectioners')
   sugar

4 tbsp good-quality cocoa powder

2 tsp vanilla extract

150 g (5 oz) cream cheese

1 tbsp coffee

whole hazelnuts, for garnish

1. Turn the oven to 175°C (345°F).
2. Whisk the eggs, sugar and vanilla until white and
   really fluffy.
3. Melt the butter, add the sour cream and coffee and
   mix it together with the eggs.
4. Mix the flour, baking powder, cocoa and salt and
   carefully fold this into the egg mixture.
5. Coarsely chop the chocolate and melt it in a water
   bath (in a bowl over boiling water). Mix this in with the
   other ingredients.
6. Pipe or spoon out the mixture onto baking paper with
   a tablespoon.
7. Bake them in batches in the middle of the oven for
   about 10 minutes. Leave them to cool completely while
   you make the Nutella frosting.

1. Mix the Nutella, icing sugar, cocoa, vanilla and cream
   cheese until creamy. Add the coffee and whip with an
   electric mixer.
2. Fill an icing bag with a round nozzle.
3. Frost the underside of one cake and put it together
   with another cake (without frosting), like a macaron.
   Put a little frosting on top and garnish each pie with a
   hazelnut.

Lemon meringue whoopie pies

20 WHOOPIE PIES

100 g (3½ oz) softened butter

150 g (5 oz) sugar

2 tsp vanilla extract

350 g (12 oz) plain (all-purpose) flour

1 tsp baking powder

1 tsp bicarbonate of soda
  (baking soda)

1 free-range egg

100 ml (3½ fl oz) double cream

1. Turn the oven to 175°C (345°F).
2. Whisk the butter, sugar and vanilla until creamy.
3. Mix the dry ingredients and fold them into the butter.
4. Add the egg and cream and mix until smooth.
5. Pipe or spoon out the mixture onto baking paper with a tablespoon.
6. Bake them, in batches, in the middle of the oven for about 10 minutes.
7. Make the lemon curd and the Italian meringue
8. Pipe lemon curd on the underside of one pie and stick it to another one, like a macaron.
9. Pipe the meringue on top of the whoopie pie and brown the meringue with a crème brûlée blowtorch.

LEMON CURD

3 lemons

150 g (5 oz) sugar

50 g (1¾ oz) butter

2 tbsp cornstarch (cornflour)

2 free-range eggs

2 free-range yolks

100 ml (3½ fl oz) double cream

1. Boil the juice from two of the lemons and the grated peel from three lemons with the sugar and butter.
2. Strain and throw away the peel.
3. Mix the cornstarch with the juice from the third lemon and add this to the warm liquid.
4. Whip the eggs and yolks.
5. Add the eggs to the mixture and put it back on the stove. Simmer while stirring until the cream has thickened.
6. Pour the curd into a bowl and leave to cool completely.
7. Whisk the cream until fluffy and mix it with the cool curd.

ITALIAN MERINGUE

3 free-range egg whites

1 pinch salt

200 g (7 oz) sugar

50 ml (1¾ fl oz) water

1. Whip the egg whites and salt until firm in a mixer. Meanwhile, boil the sugar and water into a syrup at exactly 121°C (250°F) in a little saucepan (use an electronic thermometer to check the temperature).
2. Pour the hot sugar syrup over the egg whites while whipping them. Continue whipping until the meringue is cool.

Chunky monkey cupcakes

12 CUPCAKES

2 free-range eggs

150 g (5 oz) sugar

75 g (2½ oz) butter

75 ml (2½ fl oz) milk

250 g (9 oz) plain (all-purpose) flour

2 tsp baking powder

1 pinch salt

1 tsp ground ginger

1 tsp ground cinnamon

75 g (2½ oz) good-quality 70%
  dark chocolate

3 bananas

100 g (3½ oz) whole walnuts

CHOCOLATE FROSTING

60 g (2 oz) softened butter

500 g (17½ oz) icing (confectioners')
  sugar

50 g (1¾ oz) good-quality cocoa
  powder

2 tsp vanilla extract

100 g (3½ oz) cream cheese

1 tbsp warm coffee

fresh cherries, for garnish

1. Turn the oven to 175°C (345°F).
2. Whisk the eggs and sugar until white and really fluffy.
3. Melt the butter, add the milk and mix this into the eggs.
4. Mix the flour, baking powder, salt, ginger and
   cinnamon and carefully fold this into the other
   ingredients.
5. Coarsely chop the chocolate. Mash one banana and
   slice the other two. Add the chocolate, bananas and
   walnuts to the mixture.
6. Set out paper cups in a muffin tin and fill the cups
   until two-thirds full with the mixture.
7. Bake them in the middle of the oven for about 15-20
   minutes. Leave them to cool.

1. Mix the butter, icing sugar, cocoa and vanilla until
   creamy.
2. Whisk in the cream cheese and the coffee.
3. Spread the frosting on the cupcakes and garnish with
   a cherry.

CHUNKY MONKEY IS A FLAVOUR OF ICE CREAM THAT I ALWAYS ATE WHEN I LIVED IN NEW YORK.
THE COMBINATION OF BANANA ICE CREAM, DARK CHOCOLATE AND WALNUTS IS FANTASTIC.
NOW I'VE BROUGHT THOSE FLAVOURS TOGETHER IN MY WONDERFUL CHUNKY MONKEY
CUPCAKES. YUMMY!

S'mores whoopie pies

20 WHOOPIE PIES

3 free-range eggs

250 g (9 oz) sugar

1 tsp vanilla extract

50 g (1¾ oz) butter

100 g (3½ oz) sour cream

2 tbsp cold coffee

350 g (12 oz) plain (all-purpose) flour

2 tsp baking powder

4 tbsp good-quality cocoa powder

1 pinch salt

100 g (3½ oz) good-quality 70%
  dark chocolate

FILLING

1 jar (400 g/14 oz) Nutella

1 bag marshmallows

1. Turn the oven to 175°C (345°F).
2. Whisk the eggs, sugar and vanilla until white and really fluffy.
3. Melt the butter, add the sour cream and coffee and mix with the eggs.
4. Mix the flour, baking powder, cocoa and salt and carefully fold this into the egg mixture.
5. Coarsely chop the chocolate and melt it in a water bath (in a bowl over boiling water). Add it to the other ingredients.
6. Pipe or spoon out the mixture onto baking paper with a tablespoon.
7. Bake them in batches in the middle of the oven for about 10 minutes. Leave them to cool completely.
8. Spread some Nutella on the underside of the whoopie pies. Thread the marshmallows (one or two at a time) on a skewer and grill them over a gas flame, a grill or gas burner until they have turned golden.
9. Press a grilled marshmallow into the Nutella and place the whoopie pies together like a macaron.

S'MORES ARE AN OLD AMERICAN SCOUT CLASSIC. TO MAKE THEM, YOU SQUEEZE A GRILLED MARSHMALLOW BETWEEN TWO BISCUITS (I PERSONALLY LIKE MARIE BISCUITS) TOGETHER WITH SOME CHOCOLATE CREAM OR MELTED CHOCOLATE. IT IS REALLY GOOD AND BOTH ADULTS AND KIDS USUALLY LOVE IT.

Strawberry cupcakes

12 CUPCAKES
2 free-range eggs
150 g (5 oz) sugar
1 tsp vanilla extract
75 g (2½ oz) butter
75 ml (2½ fl oz) milk
250 g (9 oz) plain (all-purpose) flour
1½ tsp baking powder
1 pinch salt
grated peel and juice from 1 lemon
300 g (10½ oz) fresh strawberries

1. Turn the oven to 175°C (345°F).
2. Whisk the eggs, sugar and vanilla until white and really fluffy.
3. Melt the butter and add the milk, then mix it into the eggs.
4. Mix the flour, baking powder and salt, and carefully fold it into the egg mixture.
5. Mix in the grated peel and lemon juice.
6. Slice the strawberries and carefully fold them into the batter.
7. Set out paper cups in a muffin tin and fill the cups until two-thirds full with the mixture.
8. Bake them in the middle of the oven for about 20 minutes. Leave them to cool.

CREAM CHEESE FROSTING
60 g (2 oz) softened butter
500 g (17½ oz) icing (confectioners') sugar
1 tsp vanilla extract
1 tbsp freshly squeezed lemon juice
100 g (3½ oz) cream cheese

fresh strawberries, for garnish

1. Whip the butter, icing sugar, vanilla, lemon juice and cream cheese until creamy.
2. Spread the frosting on the cupcakes and slice the strawberries.
3. Garnish the cakes with the strawberries.

Nutty pistachio cupcakes

12 CUPCAKES

3 free-range eggs
200 g (7 oz) sugar
200 g (7 oz) unsalted, shelled
  pistachios
150 g (5 oz) plain (all-purpose) flour
1 tsp baking powder
50 g (1¾ oz) butter
50 ml (1¾ fl oz) milk

1. Turn the oven to 175°C (345°F).
2. Whisk the eggs, sugar and vanilla until white and really fluffy.
3. Pulverise the nuts in a mixer or grind them.
4. Mix the nuts, flour and baking powder and fold into the eggs.
5. Melt the butter and mix it with the milk and fold it into the rest of the ingredients.
6. Set out paper cups in a muffin tin and fill the cups until two-thirds full with the mixture.
7. Bake them in the middle of the oven for about 20 minutes. Test with a toothpick; the cakes shouldn't be sticky. Leave them to cool.

NUTELLA FROSTING

100 g (3½ oz) Nutella
400 g (14 oz) icing (confectioners')
  sugar
4 tbsp good-quality cocoa powder
2 tsp vanilla extract
150 g (5 oz) cream cheese
1 tbsp coffee

1. Whisk the Nutella, icing sugar, cocoa, vanilla and cream cheese until creamy.
2. Add the coffee.
3. Spread the frosting on the cupcakes.

Hi-hat cupcakes

12 CUPCAKES

3 free-range eggs
250 g (9 oz) sugar
1 tsp vanilla extract
50 g (1¾ oz) butter
100 ml (3½ fl oz) sour cream
2 tbsp cold coffee
350 g (12 oz) plain (all-purpose) flour
2 tsp baking powder
4 tbsp good-quality cocoa powder
1 pinch salt
100 g (3½ oz) good-quality 70% dark chocolate

1. Turn the oven to 175°C (345°F).
2. Whisk the eggs, sugar and vanilla until white and really fluffy.
3. Melt the butter, add the sour cream and coffee and mix it with the eggs.
4. Mix the flour, baking powder, cocoa and salt, and carefully fold this into the egg mixture.
5. Coarsely chop the chocolate and melt it in a water bath (in a bowl over boiling water).
6. Add the chocolate to the other ingredients.
7. Set out paper cups in a muffin tin and fill the cups until two-thirds full with the mixture.
8. Bake them in the middle of the oven for about 15 minutes. Leave them to cool.

MERINGUE

6 free-range egg whites
850 g (29¾ oz) sugar
2 tsp vanilla extract
juice from 1 lemon

1. Mix the egg whites, sugar, vanilla and lemon juice in a stainless steel bowl.
2. Place the bowl in a water bath (over boiling water). Stir until the sugar has melted, then whip into a fluffy meringue and until there are clear tracks behind the whisk. The meringue should be about 65°C (150°F).
3. Remove the bowl from the water bath and continue to whip it (in a mixer) until it is completely cool.
4. Using an icing bag with a round nozzle, pipe the meringue into high spirals on the cupcakes.
5. Cool completely in the refrigerator before you dip them in chocolate.

CHOCOLATE TOPPING

350 g (12 oz) good-quality 70% dark chocolate
3 tbsp oil

1. Chop the chocolate and melt it in a water bath (in a bowl over boiling water) together with the oil.
2. Pour the chocolate into a little bowl and let it cool a little.
3. Remove the cupcakes from the fridge and dip each meringue top into the melted chocolate. Brush more chocolate where needed.

Raspberry coconut pie cupcakes

12 CUPCAKES
2 free-range eggs
150 g (5 oz) sugar
1 tsp vanilla extract
75 g (2½ oz) butter
50 g (1¾ oz) double cream
275 g (9½ oz) plain
 (all-purpose) flour
1½ tsp baking powder
1 pinch salt
grated peel and juice from 2 limes
500 g (17½ oz) frozen raspberries
2 tbsp plain (all-purpose) flour

COCONUT CRUMBLE
75 g (2½ oz) cold butter
50 g (1¾ oz) demerara sugar
150 g (5 oz) plain (all-purpose) flour
75 g (2½ oz) oats
75 g (2½ oz) coconut flakes
grated peel from 1-2 limes

double cream, for garnish

1. Turn the oven to 175°C (345°F).
2. Whisk the eggs, sugar and vanilla until white and really fluffy.
3. Melt the butter, add the cream and mix it into the eggs.
4. Mix the flour, baking powder and salt and carefully fold it into the egg mixture.
5. Mix in the grated peel and juice from the limes.
6. Set out paper cups in a muffin tin.
7. Mix the raspberries with the 2 tablespoons of flour.
8. Layer the batter and the raspberries in the cup. Fill the cups until two-thirds full with the mixture.
9. To make the coconut crumble, pinch together cubed butter with the sugar, flour, oats, coconut and grated lime peel.
10. Top the cupcakes with coconut crumble.
11. Bake them in the middle of the oven for about 35 minutes. Leave them to cool.
12. Whip the cream until fluffy and pipe on the cupcakes.

French meringue cupcakes

12 CUPCAKES

7 free-range egg whites
500 g (17½ oz) sugar
1 pinch salt
50 g (1¾ oz) almond flakes
100 g (3½ oz) good-quality 70%
  dark chocolate

TOPPING

400 ml (14 fl oz) double cream
1 punnet fresh raspberries
½ punnet strawberries
1 handful cherries

1. Turn the oven to 150°C (345°F).
2. Mix the egg whites, sugar and salt in a stainless steel bowl.
3. Place the bowl in a water bath (over boiling water). Stir until the sugar has melted and the meringue is about 60-65°C (140-150°F).
4. Remove the bowl from the water bath and continue to whip it in a mixer at high speed for a long time until it is completely cool.
5. Toast the almond flakes in a dry saucepan or frying pan.
6. Melt the chocolate in a water bath and fold it and the almonds into the meringue so it turns striped.
7. Spoon out the meringues in muffin cups and bake them in the oven for about 50 minutes. They should be soft and chewy in the middle.
8. Whip the cream until fluffy and spoon it onto the meringue. Garnish with fresh berries.

Chocolate mint whoopie pies

20 WHOOPIE PIES

3 free-range eggs

250 g (9 oz) sugar

1 tsp vanilla extract

50 g (1¾ oz) butter

100 ml (3½ fl oz) cream

2 tbsp cold coffee

350 g (12 oz) plain (all-purpose) flour

2 tsp baking powder

4 tbsp good-quality cocoa powder

1 pinch salt

1. Turn the oven to 175°C (345°F).
2. Whisk the eggs, sugar and vanilla until white and really fluffy.
3. Melt the butter, add the cream and coffee and mix this into the eggs.
4. Mix the flour, baking powder, cocoa and salt and carefully fold this into the other ingredients.
5. Pipe or spoon out the mixture onto baking paper with a tablespoon.
6. Bake them in batches in the middle of the oven for about 10 minutes. Leave them to cool completely while you make the mint chocolate frosting.

MINT CHOCOLATE FROSTING

60 g (2 oz) softened butter

500 g (17½ oz) icing (confectioners') sugar

50 g (1¾ oz) good-quality cocoa powder

2 tsp vanilla extract

100 g (3½ oz) cream cheese

1 tbsp warm coffee

peppermint oil, to taste

sugar roses, for garnish

1. Mix the butter, icing sugar, cocoa, vanilla and cream cheese together until creamy. Add the coffee and whip the frosting with an electric mixer. Flavour with peppermint oil.
2. Fill an icing bag with a round nozzle with the frosting.
3. Pipe the frosting onto the underside of one cake and put it together with another cake (without frosting), like a macaron. Pipe some frosting on top and garnish with a sugar rose.

Kitchen magic...

Different ovens have different temperatures, so get to know your oven. Do you need to turn the baking tray because your oven heats up unevenly? Convection ovens are more effective and they shorten the baking time in comparison with regular ovens. I've used a convection oven in my recipes.

Tip! I always bake with free-range eggs. The cupcakes taste more delicious and have a more beautiful colour. Remember that all ingredients must be fresh when you bake. You won't get good cakes from expired flour. All your tools should be clean and dry; you'll never succeed with meringue if there is water in the bowl. Never whisk the flour into the cake batter or you'll get compact cakes.

82

Double chocolate whoopie pies

20 WHOOPIE PIES

3 free-range eggs
250 g (9 oz) sugar
1 tsp vanilla extract
50 g (1¾ oz) butter
100 ml (3½ fl oz) sour cream
2 tbsp cold coffee
350 g (12 oz) plain (all-purpose) flour
2 tsp baking powder
4 tbsp good-quality cocoa powder
1 pinch salt
100 g (3½ oz) good-quality 70%
    dark chocolate

1. Turn the oven to 175°C (345°F).
2. Whisk the eggs, sugar and vanilla until white and
   really fluffy.
3. Melt the butter, add the sour cream and coffee and
   mix this into the eggs.
4. Mix the flour, baking powder, cocoa and salt and
   carefully fold this into the other ingredients.
5. Coarsely chop the chocolate and melt it in a water
   bath (in a bowl over boiling water). Mix this in to
   everything else.
6. Pipe or spoon out the mixture onto baking paper with
   a tablespoon.
7. Bake them in batches in the middle of the oven for
   about 10 minutes. Leave them to cool completely while
   you make the white chocolate frosting.

WHITE CHOCOLATE FROSTING

200 g (7 oz) good-quality white
    chocolate
200 g (7 oz) cream cheese

1. Chop the chocolate and melt it in a water bath (in a
   bowl over boiling water).
2. Whisk the chocolate with the cream cheese. Fill an
   icing bag with a round nozzle.
3. Pipe the frosting onto the underside of one cake and
   put it together with another cake (without frosting),
   like a macaron.

THE ORIGINAL WHOOPIE PIE WAS BLACK AND WHITE WITH MARSHMALLOW FLUFF IN
BETWEEN THE CAKES. THAT'S TOO SWEET FOR MY TASTE. SO THIS IS MY VERSION, WHICH IS
REMINISCENT OF OREO COOKIES.

Jane's apple pie cupcakes

12 CUPCAKES

2 free-range eggs
150 g (5 oz) sugar
1 tsp vanilla extract
75 g (2½ oz) butter
75 ml (2½ fl oz) milk
250 g (9 oz) plain (all-purpose) flour
1½ tsp baking powder
1 pinch salt
1 tsp freshly ground cardamom

double cream, for garnish

1. Turn the oven to 175°C (345°F).
2. Make the vanilla filling and apple filling (see recipes below).
3. Whisk the eggs, sugar and vanilla until white and really fluffy.
4. Melt the butter, add the milk and mix it with the eggs.
5. Mix the flour, baking powder, salt and cardamom and carefully fold this into the eggs.
6. Set out paper cups in a muffin tin and layer the batter with the apple filling until the cups are two-thirds full with the mixture.
7. Fill an icing bag with the vanilla filling. Press the icing bag into the batter and pipe a little vanilla filling into each cupcake.
8. Bake them in the middle of the oven for about 20–25 minutes. Leave them to cool.
9. Whip the cream until fluffy and pipe on the cupcakes.

VANILLA FILLING

½ vanilla pod
200 g (7 oz) cream cheese
1 tbsp icing (confectioners') sugar
1 tbsp double cream

1. Halve the vanilla pod and scrape the seeds from it.
2. Whip the cream cheese, the vanilla seeds, the icing sugar and cream until fluffy.

APPLE FILLING

3 apples
25 g (¾ oz) butter
1½ tbsp sugar
2 tsp ground cinnamon

1. Peel and de-seed the apples. Slice them into small pieces and fry them in butter, sugar and cinnamon until soft. Leave to cool.

Walnut brownie cupcakes

12 CUPCAKES

200 g (7 oz) walnuts

175 g (6 oz) butter

150 g (5 oz) sugar

150 g (5 oz) light muscovado sugar

150 g (5 oz) good-quality cocoa
  powder

50 ml (1¾ fl oz) golden syrup

1 pinch salt

3 free-range eggs

150 g (5 oz) plain (all-purpose) flour

1 tsp baking powder

100 g (3½ oz) good-quality 70%
  dark chocolate

whipped cream and fresh
  raspberries, for garnish

1. Turn the oven to 175°C (345°F).
2. Toast the whole walnuts in a hot and dry frying pan.
3. Whip the butter, sugar and muscovado sugar until creamy.
4. Add the cocoa, syrup and salt.
5. Whisk in one egg at a time.
6. Mix the flour with the baking powder and sift it into the other ingredients.
7. Coarsely chop the chocolate and add it and the whole walnuts to the batter.
8. Set out paper cups in a muffin tin and fill the cups until two-thirds full with the mixture.
9. Bake them in the middle of the oven for about 15-20 minutes. Test them with a toothpick; they should be a little sticky in the middle. Leave them to cool.
10. Garnish the cupcakes with lightly whipped cream and fresh raspberries.

MY BROWNIE CUPCAKES SHOULD BE A LITTLE STICKY IN THE MIDDLE. YOU SHOULD THEREFORE BE CAREFUL NOT TO BAKE THEM TOO LONG. EXACTLY HOW LONG THEY SHOULD BE BAKED VARIES FROM OVEN TO OVEN, SO THE SIMPLEST WAY TO MAKE SURE THEY DON'T GET DRY IN THE MIDDLE IS TO TEST THEM WITH A TOOTHPICK OR SIMILAR. IT SHOULD BE A LITTLE STICKY.

Nutella cupcakes

12 CUPCAKES

3 free-range eggs
250 g (9 oz) sugar
1 tsp vanilla extract
100 g (3½ oz) butter
100 ml (3½ fl oz) milk
350 g (12 oz) plain (all-purpose) flour
2 tsp baking powder
1 pinch salt
grated peel and juice from 1 lemon

TOPPING

1 jar (250 g/9 oz) Nutella
sprinkles, for garnish

1. Turn the oven to 175°C (345°F).
2. Whisk the eggs, sugar and vanilla until white and really fluffy.
3. Melt the butter, add the milk and mix this into the eggs.
4. Mix the flour, baking powder and salt and carefully fold into the other ingredients.
5. Mix in the grated lemon peel and juice from one lemon.
6. Set out paper cups in a muffin tin and fill the cups until two-thirds full with the mixture.
7. Bake them in the middle of the oven for about 15 minutes. Leave them to cool completely.
8. Spread Nutella on the cupcakes and top with sprinkles.

Elvis Presley's cupcakes

12 CUPCAKES

3 free-range eggs

250 g (9 oz) sugar

1 tsp vanilla extract

50 g (1¾ oz) butter

100 ml (3½ fl oz) sour cream

350 g (12 oz) plain (all-purpose) flour

1 tsp baking powder

1 pinch salt

100 g (3½ oz) good-quality 70%
  dark chocolate

4 tbsp good-quality cocoa powder

2 tbsp cold coffee

3 bananas

200 g (7 oz) salted peanuts

1. Turn the oven to 175°C (345°F).
2. Whisk the eggs, sugar and vanilla until white and really fluffy.
3. Melt the butter, add the sour cream and mix this into the eggs.
4. Mix the flour, baking powder and salt and carefully fold into the other ingredients.
5. Coarsely chop the chocolate and melt it in a water bath (in a bowl over boiling water).
6. Add the chocolate, cocoa and coffee to the batter.
7. Mash one of the bananas and add it. Slice the other two.
8. Set out paper cups in a muffin tin.
9. Chop the peanuts and layer them with batter and banana slices in the muffin cups until the cups are two-thirds full with the mixture.
10. Bake them in the middle of the oven for about 15-20 minutes. Leave them to cool completely.

PEANUT BUTTER FROSTING

50 g (1¾ oz) softened peanut butter

250 g (9 oz) icing (confectioners')
  sugar

2 tbsp good-quality cocoa powder

1 tsp vanilla extract

100 g (3½ oz) cream cheese

1 tbsp warm coffee

salted peanuts, for garnish

1. Mix the peanut butter, icing sugar, cocoa, vanilla and cream cheese until creamy.
2. Add the coffee and whip with an electric mixer.
3. Spread the frosting on the cupcakes and garnish with peanuts.

Coconut cream cupcakes

12 CUPCAKES

3 free-range eggs

250 g (9 oz) sugar

1 tsp vanilla extract

75 g (2½ oz) butter

100 ml (3½ fl oz) coconut cream

350 g (12 oz) plain (all-purpose) flour

1 tsp baking powder

1 pinch salt

1. Turn the oven to 175°C (345°F).
2. Whisk the eggs, sugar and vanilla until white and really fluffy.
3. Melt the butter, add the coconut cream and mix this into the eggs.
4. Mix the flour, baking powder and salt and carefully fold into the other ingredients.
5. Set out paper cups in a muffin tin and fill the cups until two-thirds full with the mixture.
6. Bake them in the middle of the oven for about 15-20 minutes. Leave them to cool.

COCONUT CREAM FROSTING

60 g (2 oz) softened butter

*400 g (14 oz) icing (confectioners')
  sugar*

2 tsp vanilla extract

1-2 tbsp Malibu (coconut liqueur)

100 g (3½ oz) cream cheese

*grated coconut or coconut flakes,
  for garnish*

1. Whisk the butter, icing sugar, vanilla, coconut liqueur and cream cheese until creamy.
2. Spread the frosting onto the cupcakes and garnish with coconut.

COCONUT CREAM IS THE FATTIER VERSION OF COCONUT MILK. YOU CAN ALSO USE THE
THICKER PART OF COCONUT MILK THAT USUALLY SETTLES ON TOP OF THE MILK IN THE TIN.
IF YOU WANT, YOU CAN REPLACE THE COCONUT LIQUEUR WITH COCONUT EXTRACT, WHICH
YOU CAN BUY IN WELL-STOCKED GROCERY STORES OR ORDER ONLINE.

Chocolate!

»too much of a good thing
can be wonderful«

After eight cupcakes

12 CUPCAKES

3 free-range eggs

250 g (9 oz) sugar

1 tsp vanilla extract

50 g (1¾ oz) butter

100 ml (3½ oz) sour cream

2 tbsp coffee

350 g (12 oz) plain (all-purpose) flour

2 tsp baking powder

4 tbsp good-quality cocoa

1 pinch salt

100 g (3½ oz) good-quality 70% dark chocolate

24 pieces (250 g/9 oz) After Eight chocolates

1. Turn the oven to 175°C (345°F).
2. Whisk the eggs, sugar and vanilla until white and really fluffy.
3. Melt the butter, add the sour cream and coffee.
4. Mix the flour, baking powder, cocoa and salt and carefully fold into the other ingredients.
5. Coarsely chop the chocolate and melt it in a water bath (in a bowl over boiling water).
6. Add the chocolate to the batter.
7. Set out paper cups in a muffin tin and fill the cups until two-thirds full with the mixture.
8. Break the After Eights and press one into each cupcake.
9. Bake them in the middle of the oven for about 15 minutes. Leave them to cool.

MINT CREAM FROSTING

150 ml (5 fl oz) double cream

50 ml (1¾ fl oz) milk

50 ml (1¾ fl oz) honey

150 g (5 oz) good-quality 70% dark chocolate

peppermint oil, to taste

1. Boil the cream, milk and honey in a saucepan. Remove from the heat and leave to cool a little.
2. Finely chop the chocolate and melt it into the cream.
3. Flavour as desired with peppermint oil.
4. Frost the cakes using an icing bag with a round nozzle.

THIS IS PROBABLY MY FAVOURITE FLAVOUR. I HAVE ALWAYS LOVED MINT CHOCOLATE! IF YOU WANT TO MAKE A SIMPLER VERSION OF THIS WONDERFUL CUPCAKE, YOU CAN SKIP THE MINT CHOCOLATE FROSTING AND PLACE AN AFTER EIGHT ON TOP OF EACH CUPCAKE AFTER YOU TAKE THEM OUT OF THE OVEN. IT MELTS INTO A SORT OF GLAZE ON THE CUPCAKES.

Hazelnut cupcakes

12 CUPCAKES

2 free-range eggs

150 g (5 oz) sugar

100 g (3½ oz) hazelnuts

100 g (3½ oz) good-quality 70%
  dark chocolate

150 g (5 oz) plain (all-purpose) flour

1 tsp baking powder

50 ml (1¾ fl oz) double cream

1. Turn the oven to 175°C (345°F).
2. Whisk the eggs and sugar until white and really fluffy.
3. Pulverise the nuts in a mixer or grind them.
4. Coarsely chop the chocolate.
5. Mix the nuts, chocolate, flour and baking powder and
   fold into the other ingredients.
6. Add the cream.
7. Set out paper cups in a muffin tin and fill the cups until
   two-thirds full with the mixture.
8. Bake them in the middle of the oven for about
   15 minutes. Test them with a toothpick; they shouldn't
   be sticky. Leave them to cool.

NUTELLA FROSTING

100 g (3½ oz) Nutella

400 g (14 oz) icing (confectioners')
  sugar

4 tbsp good-quality cocoa

2 tsp vanilla extract

150 g (5 oz) cream cheese

1 tbsp coffee

1-2 tbsp Frangelico (hazelnut
  liqueur)

hazelnuts, for garnish

1. Mix the Nutella, icing sugar, cocoa, vanilla and cream
   cheese until creamy.
2. Add the coffee and Frangelico and whip until fluffy.
3. Spread the frosting on the cupcakes and garnish with
   a hazelnut.

Lime and raspberry cupcakes

12 CUPCAKES

3 free-range eggs
250 g (9 oz) sugar
1 tsp vanilla extract
100 g (3½ oz) butter
100 ml (3½ fl oz) milk
400 g (14 oz) plain (all-purpose) flour
2 tsp baking powder
1 pinch salt
100 g (3½ oz) poppy seeds
grated peel and juice from 5 limes

whipped cream and fresh
  raspberries, for garnish

1. Turn the oven to 175°C (345°F).
2. Whisk the eggs, sugar and vanilla until white and
   really fluffy.
3. Melt the butter, add the milk and mix this into the eggs.
4. Mix the flour, baking powder, salt and poppy seeds
   and carefully fold into the other ingredients.
5. Add the grated peel and juice from five limes.
6. Set out paper cups in a muffin tin and fill the cups
   until two-thirds full with the mixture.
7. Bake them in the middle of the oven for about
   15 minutes. Leave them to cool completely.
8. Pipe whipped cream on each cupcake and garnish
   with raspberries.

Almond pavlova cupcakes

12 CUPCAKES

7 free-range egg whites
525 g (18¼ oz) sugar
juice from ½ lemon
50 g (1¾ oz) flaked almonds

TOPPING

500 ml (17 fl oz) double cream
300 ml (10½ fl oz) Greek yoghurt
3 tbsp icing (confectioners') sugar
1 litre (36 fl oz) fresh berries

1. Turn the oven to 150°C (300°F).
2. Mix the egg whites, sugar and lemon juice in a
   stainless steel bowl. Stir until the sugar has melted.
3. Place the bowl in a water bath (over boiling water) and
   whisk until the meringue is about 60-65°C (140-150°F).
4. Remove the bowl from the water bath and continue to
   whip it with a mixer until it is cool.
5. Carefully fold the almonds into the meringue.
6. Set out paper cups in a muffin tin and fill the cups
   until two-thirds full with the meringue.
7. Bake them in the middle of the oven for about 40-55
   minutes. They should be a little chewy and soft in the
   middle.
8. Whip the cream for the topping and mix it with the
   yoghurt and icing sugar. Spoon it over the meringues.
9. Garnish each cupcake with berries.

ALMOND PAVLOVA CUPCAKES

Bunting ... All you need to make your own bunting is cotton rope and some scrap material (ideally in different colours and patterns). Cut the cloth into triangles and pin them to the rope. Take out your sewing machine and sew the triangles with straight or zigzag seams. If you want to cheat and make it out of paper, cut some nice paper in different colours into triangles and staple them to a rope.

Party
PRINCESS

Sweet and simple...

I nearly always choose a theme for my parties. It's so much easier and more fun to decorate, set the table and bake! Often, I make sure there are a lot of colours and I mix different chairs, tablecloths and napkins. You can set the table under a parasol, a sailcloth, a pretty tent or a piece of material decorated with bunting. Then you feel as though you're snug inside something and it's cosier. If you're inside the house, you can hang up flags, lamps or balloons over the table.

Tip! If you are putting together different tables (round and rectangular), it's really attractive to mix flowered, checked and spotted tablecloths.

Passionfruit meringue cupcakes

12 CUPCAKES

2 free-range eggs

150 g (5 oz) sugar

1 tsp vanilla extract

75 g (2½ oz) butter

75 ml (2½ fl oz) double cream

250 g (9 oz) plain (all-purpose) flour

1½ tsp baking powder

1 pinch salt

1. Turn the oven to 175°C (345°F).
2. Whisk the eggs, sugar and vanilla until white and really fluffy.
3. Melt the butter, add the cream and mix this into the eggs.
4. Mix the flour, baking powder and salt and carefully fold into the other ingredients.
5. Set out paper cups in a muffin tin and fill the cups until two-thirds full with the mixture. Bake them, in the middle of the oven, for about 15 minutes. Leave them to cool.
6. Cut the top off the cupcakes using a knife at a 45-degree angle so the cakes are scooped out a little.
7. Fill the hole with passionfruit curd and top with meringue. Brown the meringue with a crème brûlée blowtorch.

PASSIONFRUIT CURD

10 fresh passionfruits
   (about 150 ml/5 fl oz liquid)

grated peel and juice from 1 lime

150 g (5 oz) sugar

25 g (¾ oz) butter

1½ tbsp cornstarch (cornflour)

1 free-range egg

1 free-range yolk

75 ml (2½ fl oz) double cream

1. Scrape out the juice and seeds from the passionfruits and strain the juice. Throw away the seeds.
2. Boil two-thirds of the passionfruit juice with the grated lime peel, lime juice, sugar and butter. Remove from the heat.
3. Mix the cornstarch with the remaining one-third of the passionfruit juice and whisk it into the warm liquid.
4. Whisk the egg and yolk and add to the liquid. Put back on the stove and simmer while stirring until the cream has thickened. Strain into a bowl and leave to cool completely.
5. Whip the cream until fluffy and mix it with the passionfruit cream. Put somewhere cold.

ITALIAN MERINGUE

3 free-range egg whites

1 pinch salt

200 g (7 oz) sugar

50 ml (1¾ fl oz) water

2. Whisk the egg whites and salt until firm. Meanwhile, boil the sugar and water into a syrup at exactly 121°C (250°F) in a little saucepan (use an electronic thermometer to check the temperature).
3. Pour hot sugar syrup over the egg whites while whipping them at medium speed. Continue whipping until the meringue is cool.

Ginger raspberry whoopie pies

20 WHOOPIE PIES

100 g (3½ oz) softened butter

150 g (5 oz) sugar

350 g (12 oz) plain (all-purpose) flour

2 tsp vanilla extract

1 tsp ground ginger

1 tsp baking powder

1 tsp bicarbonate of soda (baking
  powder)

1 free-range egg

100 ml (3½ fl oz) double cream

1. Turn the oven to 175°C (345°F).
2. Whisk the butter and sugar until creamy.
3. Mix the dry ingredients together and add to the butter.
4. Add the egg and cream and stir into a smooth batter.
5. Pipe or spoon out the mixture onto baking paper with
   a tablespoon.
6. Bake them in batches in the middle of the oven for
   about 10 minutes. Leave them to cool completely

RASPBERRY FROSTING

300 g (10½ oz) icing
  (confectioners') sugar

150 g (5 oz) cream cheese

150 g (5 oz) fresh raspberries

1. Mix the icing sugar and cream cheese until creamy.
2. Carefully fold in the raspberries and spread the
   frosting onto the underside of one cake and put it
   together with another cake (without frosting), like a
   macaron.

IT IS DELICIOUS TO FLAVOUR FROSTING WITH VARIOUS FRESH BERRIES. CAREFULLY CRUSH THEM
WITH THE FROSTING SO THAT IT TAKES ON A LITTLE COLOUR. IT'S IMPORTANT NOT TO MASH THEM
TOO MUCH OR ELSE THERE'S A RISK THAT THE FROSTING WILL BE TOO RUNNY FROM THE LIQUID
IN THE BERRIES. I DON'T USE FROZEN BERRIES BECAUSE THEY USUALLY RELEASE LIQUID WHEN
THEY DEFROST.

Madeleine whoopie pies

30 WHOOPIE PIES

75 g (2½ oz) softened butter

75 g (2½ oz) sugar

1 tsp vanilla extract

grated peel from 1 lemon

2 free-range eggs

150 g (5 oz) plain (all-purpose) flour

1 tsp baking powder

softened butter, for the tin

1. Turn the oven to 175°C (345°F).
2. Whisk the butter, sugar, vanilla and grated lemon peel until light and creamy.
3. Mix in the eggs, flour and baking powder and add to the batter.
4. Brush the madeleine tin (preferably a small model) thoroughly with softened butter.
5. Pipe the batter into the tins and place them on the metal rack. Set the rack in the oven and bake the biscuits in batches for about 8 minutes, until golden.

STRAWBERRY FROSTING

60 g (2 oz) softened butter

400 g (14 oz) icing (confectioners') sugar

150 g (5 oz) cream cheese

1 tsp vanilla extract

100 g (3½ oz) finely cubed strawberries

1. Mix the butter, icing sugar, cream cheese and vanilla until creamy.
2. Add the strawberries and put the frosting in the refrigerator for a little while until it firms up.
3. Pipe the frosting onto the underside of one madeleine and put it together with another madeleine (without frosting), like a macaron.

MADELEINES ARE CLASSIC FRENCH BISCUITS. TO BAKE THEM, YOU NEED A MADELEINE TIN, WHICH IS SHELL-SHAPED (AND HERE I USE A SMALL TIN). YOU HAVE TO GREASE THE TIN THOROUGHLY WITH SOFTENED BUTTER SO YOU CAN GET THE BISCUITS OUT. THESE WHOOPIE PIES ARE MAGICAL WITH THEIR STRAWBERRY FROSTING.

Wedding cupcakes

24 CUPCAKES
6 free-range eggs
500 g (17½ oz) sugar
2 tsp vanilla extract
200 g (7 oz) butter
200 ml (7 fl oz) milk
700 g (1 lb 9 oz) plain (all-purpose) flour
4 tsp baking powder
1 pinch salt
grated peel from 2 and juice from 1 lemons

1. Turn the oven to 175°C (345°F).
2. Whisk the eggs, sugar and vanilla until white and really fluffy.
3. Melt the butter, add the milk and mix this into the eggs.
4. Mix the flour, baking powder and salt and carefully fold into the other ingredients.
5. Add the grated peel from two lemons and the juice from one.
6. Set out paper cups in a muffin tin and fill the cups until two-thirds full with the mixture.
7. Bake them in the middle of the oven for about 15 minutes. Leave them to cool.

DARK CHOCOLATE MOUSSE
200 g (7 oz) good-quality 70% dark chocolate
4 free-range yolks
2 tbsp dark muscovado sugar
1 tbsp warm coffee
2 tbsp dark rum
300 ml (10½ fl oz) double cream
1 punnet fresh raspberries

1. Coarsely chop the chocolate and melt it in a water bath (in a bowl over boiling water).
2. Whisk the yolks with the muscovado sugar until creamy.
3. Add the coffee and rum, then the warm, melted chocolate.
4. Fold together with lightly whipped cream.
5. Slice off the tops of the cupcakes and scoop them out somewhat. Fill them three-quarters of the way with chocolate mousse and press in a raspberry. Put the top back on.

WHITE CHOCOLATE FROSTING
600 g (21 oz) good-quality white chocolate
600 g (21 oz) cream cheese

1. Chop the white chocolate and melt it in a water bath.
2. Whisk the chocolate with the cream cheese into a creamy frosting.
3. Spread the frosting on the cupcakes and garnish with a sugar rose.

sugar roses, for garnish

Classic cupcakes

12 CUPCAKES

3 free-range eggs

250 g (9 oz) sugar

1 tsp vanilla extract

100 g (3½ oz) butter

100 ml (3½ fl oz) milk

350 g (12 oz) plain (all-purpose) flour

2 tsp baking powder

1 pinch salt

grated peel and juice from 1 lemon

1. Turn the oven to 175°C (345°F).
2. Whisk the eggs, sugar and vanilla until white and really fluffy.
3. Melt the butter, add the milk and mix this into the eggs.
4. Mix the flour, baking powder and salt and carefully fold into the other ingredients.
5. Mix in the grated peel and juice from one lemon.
6. Set out paper cups in a muffin tin and fill the cups until two-thirds full with the mixture.
7. Bake them in the middle of the oven for about 15 minutes. Leave them to cool.

CREAM CHEESE FROSTING

60 g (2 oz) softened butter

500 g (17½ oz) icing (confectioners') sugar

1 tsp vanilla extract

1 tbsp freshly squeezed lemon juice

100 g (3½ oz) cream cheese

sprinkles or flowers, for garnish

1. Mix the butter, icing sugar, vanilla, lemon juice and cream cheese until creamy.
2. Spread the frosting on the cakes and garnish with sprinkles or flowers.

I SOMETIMES COLOUR CLASSIC CUPCAKES IN VARIOUS PASTEL COLOURS. BE CAREFUL THAT THE FROSTING DOESN'T GET TOO INTENSELY COLOURED. A COUPLE OF DROPS OF COLOURING IS ENOUGH. THEN I GARNISH THEM WITH DIFFERENT TYPES OF SPRINKLES AND OTHER NICE DECORATIONS. YOUR IMAGINATION IS THE LIMIT FOR WHAT YOU CAN DO WITH THESE CUPCAKES, AS THEY CAN BE VARIED ENDLESSLY.

Vanilla cat cupcakes

12 CUPCAKES
3 free-range eggs
250 g (9 oz) sugar
2 tsp vanilla extract
100 g (3½ oz) butter
100 ml (3½ fl oz) milk
350 g (12 oz) plain (all-purpose) flour
2 tsp baking powder
1 pinch salt
grated peel and juice from 1 lemon

1. Turn the oven to 175°C (345°F).
2. Whisk the eggs, sugar and vanilla until white and really fluffy.
3. Melt the butter, add the milk and mix this into the eggs.
4. Mix the flour, baking powder and salt and carefully fold into the other ingredients.
5. Mix in the grated peel and juice from one lemon.
6. Set out paper cups in a muffin tin and fill the cups until two-thirds full with the mixture.
7. Bake them in the middle of the oven for about 15 minutes. Leave them to cool.

CREAM CHEESE FROSTING
60 g (2 oz) softened butter
400 g (14 oz) icing (confectioners') sugar
2 tsp vanilla extract
100 g (3½ oz) cream cheese

1 tbsp good-quality cocoa

Smarties or M&M's
raspberry shoelaces
After Eights

1. Mix the butter, icing sugar, vanilla, and cream cheese and whip until really fluffy.
2. Put one-third of the frosting in another bowl and add the cocoa so it turns brown. Put it in an icing bag with a round nozzle.
3. Spread the white frosting on the cupcakes and pipe a nose out of the chocolate frosting. Place a Smartie on the nose and slice some whiskers out of the raspberry shoelaces and put them by the nose.
4. Place two Smarties as eyes. Cut the corners off an After Eight and use them as ears.

THESE LITTLE KITTIES ARE SO CUTE, AREN'T THEY? SMALL, CUTE ANIMAL CUPCAKES ARE USUALLY UNBELIEVABLY POPULAR AMONGST THE YOUNGER CROWD. ESPECIALLY IF THEY GET TO HELP IN THE KITCHEN!

Chocolate whoopie pies

20 WHOOPIE PIES

3 free-range eggs
250 g (9 oz) sugar
1 tsp vanilla extract
50 g (1¾ oz) butter
100 ml (3½ fl oz) sour cream
2 tbsp cold coffee
350 g (12 oz) plain (all-purpose) flour
2 tsp baking powder
4 tbsp good-quality cocoa
1 pinch salt
100 g (3½ oz) good-quality 70%
  dark chocolate

CHOCOLATE FROSTING

60 g (2 oz) softened butter
500 g (17½ oz) icing sugar
1 tsp vanilla extract
50 g (1¾ oz) good-quality cocoa
100 g (3½ oz) cream cheese
1 tbsp warm coffee

sugar roses and sprinkles, as
  garnish

1. Turn the oven to 175°C (345°F).
2. Whisk the eggs, sugar and vanilla until white and really fluffy.
3. Melt the butter, add the sour cream and mix this into the eggs.
4. Mix the flour, baking powder, cocoa and salt and carefully fold into the other ingredients.
5. Coarsely chop the chocolate and melt it in a water bath (in a bowl over boiling water). Add it to the batter.
6. Pipe or spoon out the mixture onto baking paper with a tablespoon.
7. Bake them in batches in the middle of the oven for about 10 minutes.

1. Mix the butter, icing sugar, vanilla, cocoa and cream cheese until creamy. Add the coffee and whip until fluffy with an electric mixer.
2. Pipe the frosting onto the underside of one cake and put it together with another cake (without frosting), like a macaron. Pipe some frosting on top and garnish with a sugar rose and some sprinkles.

Miss Piggy cupcakes

12 CUPCAKES

3 free-range eggs

250 g (9 oz) sugar

1 tsp vanilla extract

100 g (3½ oz) butter

100 ml (3½ fl oz) milk

350 g (12 oz) plain (all-purpose) flour

1 tsp baking powder

1 pinch salt

grated peel and juice from 1 lemon

1 tbsp rose water

1. Turn the oven to 175°C (345°F).
2. Whisk the eggs, sugar and vanilla until white and really fluffy.
3. Melt the butter, add the milk and mix this into the eggs.
4. Mix the flour, baking powder and salt and carefully fold into the other ingredients.
5. Add the grated peel and juice from the lemon. Add the rose water.
6. Set out paper cups in a muffin tin and fill the cups until two-thirds full with the mixture.
7. Bake them in the middle of the oven for about 15 minutes. Leave them to cool.

PINK CREAM CHEESE FROSTING

60 g (2 oz) softened butter

400 g (14 oz) icing (confectioners') sugar

1 tsp vanilla extract

1 tbsp freshly squeezed lemon juice

100 g (3½ oz) cream cheese

a couple of drops of red colouring

marshmallows

flower sprinkles

Smarties or M&M's

marzipan or sugar paste

1. Mix the butter, icing sugar, vanilla, lemon juice and cream cheese until creamy.
2. Colour the frosting with a couple of drops of colouring.
3. Spread the frosting on the cakes and garnish with a half marshmallow as a snout and add two sprinkles. Use Smarties for the eyes and roll out a little marzipan or sugar paste and cut it into ear shapes.

SERVING MISS PIGGY CUPCAKES AT A PARTY IS A GUARANTEED SUCCESS. SINCE SHE'S ALWAYS WELL-DRESSED AND PERFUMED, I'VE ADDED SOME ROSE WATER. IT'S REALLY GOOD AND IT GIVES THE CUPCAKES A FLORAL TASTE. OF COURSE, YOU CAN ALSO LEAVE IT OUT IF YOU PREFER.

White princess cupcakes

12 CUPCAKES

3 free-range eggs

250 g (9 oz) sugar

1 tsp vanilla extract

100 g (3½ oz) butter

100 ml (3½ fl oz) milk

350 g (12 oz) plain (all-purpose) flour

2 tsp baking powder

1 pinch salt

grated peel and juice from 1 lemon

1. Turn the oven to 175°C (345°F).
2. Whisk the eggs, sugar and vanilla until white and really fluffy.
3. Melt the butter, add the milk and mix this into the eggs.
4. Mix the flour, baking powder and salt and carefully fold into the other ingredients.
5. Add the grated peel and juice from the lemon.
6. Set out paper cups in a muffin tin and fill the cups until two-thirds full with the mixture.
7. Bake them in the middle of the oven for about 15 minutes. Leave them to cool.

VANILLA CREAM

500 ml (17½ fl oz) milk

1 vanilla pod

150 g (5 oz) sugar

7 free-range yolks

75 g (2½ oz) cornstarch (cornflour)

50 g (1¾ oz) softened butter

150 ml (5 fl oz) double cream

1. Boil the milk together with a vanilla pod that has been halved, with the seeds scraped out and into the milk. Take the pod out after boiling the milk.
2. Whip the sugar, yolks and cornstarch until white and fluffy.
3. Carefully add the milk, while still whipping.
4. Pour the mixture back into the saucepan and simmer while whipping hard. Pour into a cold bowl once it's thickened.
5. Melt the butter and add it to the cream while whipping it. Continue to whip until the cream is smooth.
6. Chill the vanilla cream in an ice bath or the refrigerator.
7. Whip the cream and fold it with the vanilla cream.

RASPBERRIES

500 g (17½ oz) fresh or frozen raspberries

50–100 g (1¾–3½ oz) sugar

grated peel from 2 limes

600 ml (21 oz) double cream

sugar or marzipan roses, for garnish

1. Mix the raspberries, sugar and grated lime peel in a bowl. Strain away excess liquid.
2. Slice the top off each cupcake and scoop out some of the cake with a teaspoon.
3. Place some raspberries in each hole and top with vanilla cream. Put the top back on.
4. Whip the cream until firm and fluffy and pipe it onto the tops of the cupcakes. Garnish with a sugar or marzipan rose on each.

Bling whoopie pies

20 WHOOPIE PIES
100 g (3½ oz) softened butter
150 g (5 oz) sugar
2 tsp vanilla extract
350 g (12 oz) plain (all-purpose) flour
1 tsp baking powder
1 tsp bicarbonate of soda (baking soda)
1 free-range egg
100 ml (3½ fl oz) double cream

1. Turn the oven to 175°C (345°F).
2. Whisk the butter, sugar and vanilla until creamy.
3. Add all the dry ingredients and mix well.
4. Mix in the egg and cream and stir until smooth.
5. Pipe or spoon out the mixture onto baking paper with a tablespoon.
6. Bake them in batches in the middle of the oven for about 10 minutes.

WHITE CHOCOLATE FROSTING
200 g (7 oz) good-quality white chocolate
200 g (7 oz) cream cheese

silver balls and gold-coated chocolate, for garnish

1. Chop the chocolate and melt it in a water bath (in a bowl over boiling water). Leave to cool.
2. Mix the chocolate with the cream cheese. Put the frosting in an icing bag with a star nozzle.
3. Pipe the frosting onto the underside of one cake and put it together with another cake (without frosting), like a macaron.
4. Pipe a little frosting on top of each whoopie pie, sprinkle with silver balls and place a gold-coated chocolate on each as garnish.

I ORDER GOLD-COATED CHOCOLATES OVER THE INTERNET OR GET THEM FROM WELL-STOCKED SWEET SHOPS. YOU CAN ALSO MAKE BLING WHOOPIE PIES WITH OTHER DECORATIONS, SUCH AS SUGAR ROSES, OR YOU CAN JUST USE SILVER BALLS.